BASEBALL
ALL·STARS

This book is available in quantity at special discounts for your group or organization. For further information, contact:

Triumph Books LLC
814 North Franklin Street
Chicago, Illinois 60610
(312) 337-0747

www.triumphbooks.com
Printed in U.S.A.

ISBN: 978-1-60078-832-1

Content packaged by Mojo Media, Inc.
Joe Funk: Editor
Jason Hinman: Creative Director

Interior photos courtesy of AP Images

Cover photos courtesy of Getty Images

#24

"Miguel has long been one of the most accomplished hitters in the game, and this recognition is one that he will be able to cherish for the rest of his career."

—MLB Commissioner Bud Selig commenting on Cabrera's Triple Crown

Miguel Cabrera

Statistics

Full name:
José Miguel Cabrera

Ht: 6'4" · **Wt:** 240

Hometown/Club: Maracay, Venezuela/Detroit Tigers

DOB: April 18, 1983

Position: Third base

Salary: $21,000,000

Bats/Throws: Right/Right

Fast stat: .330/44/139: Miguel's Triple Crown–winning batting average, home runs, and RBI.

Did you know?: Miguel is the first player to win baseball's Triple Crown since Boston's Carl Yastrzemski in 1967.

As a kid: Miguel's backyard bordered Maracay's baseball stadium, where he hopped the fence to watch games.

Favorite foods/fun tidbit: Miguel's parents met at a baseball field. His dad was an excellent amateur player and his mom played softball for Venezuela's national team for 14 years.

Fun fact: Miguel has driven in at least 100 runs for each of the last nine years.

Fun fact: 20: Miguel was just 20 when he entered the major leagues; he has been considered an MVP-caliber player since his debut.

Favorite music: Miguel enjoys rap. His walk-up music is currently a song by Jay-Z and Kanye West.

Biography

The first Triple Crown winner in baseball since 1967, Miguel Cabrera is statistically the best hitter in baseball today. A seven-time All-Star and a unique talent, Cabrera can play all over the field on defense and hit the ball anywhere in the ballpark when he's at the plate.

Only 20 years old when he made his big-league debut, Cabrera immediately established himself in the major leagues by hitting a walk-off home run in his first game. The 2003 Florida Marlins used Cabrera as their cleanup hitter, riding their hot rookie all the way to a World Series championship.

Cabrera showed that his strong rookie campaign was no fluke, returning to the Marlins to hit 33 home runs and drive in 112 runs on a depleted team. He made his first All-Star appearance that year and was already known as one of the best hitters in baseball. After making four straight All-Star appearances with the Marlins, he was traded to the Detroit Tigers and signed an eight-year deal with the team.

He entered the American League with a bang, belting a league-best 37 homers in his first season in Detroit. He made his fifth All-Star Game in 2010, hitting .328 and notching 38 home runs for the season.

It was clear that Cabrera was going to be the most likely candidate to win a Triple Crown, if any player actually could accomplish the feat. No man had done so since Carl Yastrzemski in 1967 and the goal seemed like one of baseball's untouchable marks.

Set up perfectly for 2012 with the Tigers acquisition of Prince Fielder, Cabrera went on a tear. It took until the last day of the season for him to clinch the Triple Crown, but his .330 batting average, 44 home runs, and 139 RBI were enough to secure Cabrera's place as one of the best hitters of all-time. Though Cabrera played well in the playoffs and hit a home run in the deciding Game 4 of the World Series, his Tigers fell short. Still, with players like Cabrera, the team is set up for many more years of contention.

> *"I only saw him pitch live one time, and it was one of the coolest things I've ever seen."*
> —fellow major league pitcher Derek Lowe

#35

Justin Verlander

Statistics

Full name:
Justin Brooks Verlander

Ht: 6'5" • **Wt:** 225

Hometown/Club: Richmond, VA/ Detroit Tigers

DOB: February 20, 1983

Position: Pitcher

Salary: $20,000,000

Bats/Throws: Right/Right

Fast stat: 2: Justin has thrown two no-hitters in his career.

Did you know?: Justin's favorite pitch to throw when he has two strikes on a hitter is his curveball.

As a kid: When he got to high school, Justin could already throw 84 miles per hour.

Favorite foods/fun tidbit:
Justin and former Brooklyn Dodgers great Don Newcombe are the only players to win the Rookie of the Year, Cy Young, and MVP awards in their careers.

Fun fact: 24: Justin's 24 wins in 2011 were the most in the majors since 1990.

Fun fact: When Justin won his Cy Young in 2011, no other pitcher received a single first-place vote.

Favorite food: Justin eats Taco Bell before every game.

Biography

Perhaps the most dominant pitcher in the game today, Justin Verlander's heat is legendary. A Cy Young winner who is a threat to throw a no-hitter every time he takes the mound, Verlander is a unique talent that has been performing at an ace's level since his first call-up to the big leagues.

His first full season in 2006 provided a sign of things to come for the talented young pitcher, as he went 17–9 and recorded a 3.63 ERA for an excellent Tigers team. The big righty quickly became famous for his velocity, recording many pitches over 100 miles per hour in every start. He started the first game of the World Series, a tremendous honor for the rookie.

Verlander stayed hot in 2007, topping his win total from his rookie year by notching 18. He threw his first career no-hitter, reaching speeds up to 102 miles per hour on his fastball as he dominated the Milwaukee Brewers. He was named to his first All-Star Game, and has missed the honor just once since then.

After taking a step back in 2008, Verlander was back on top of his game in 2009 as he won 19 games. Another 18 wins followed in 2010, setting up the right hander for a great 2011. He threw his second career no-hitter on May 7, just missing out on a perfect game. No one came close to matching Verlander's dominance in 2011, as he won the pitching Triple Crown with 24 wins, 250 strikeouts, and a 2.40 ERA.

Verlander was an All-Star yet again in 2012, winning 17 games and leading the Tigers to another World Series berth. After starting the playoffs hot, he struggled in the World Series and the Tigers were swept by the San Francisco Giants. Verlander remains one of the game's best pitchers, however, and having been close twice, it will be no surprise to see him and his Tigers teammates one day hoisting the World Series trophy.

BASEBALL ALL-STARS

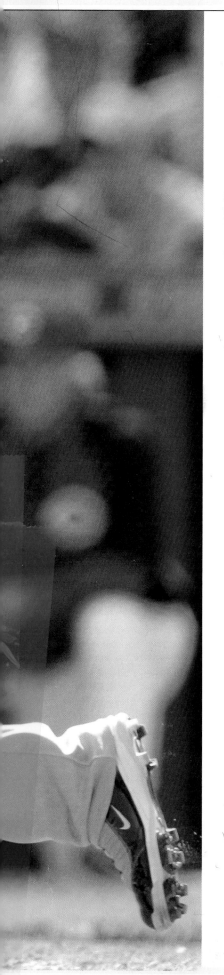

> "With my swing, there's nothing that can really change. It's different from a lefty's swing, which is kind of long and loopy. Me, I'm short and quick."
>
> —Andrew McCutchen

Andrew McCutchen

Statistics

Full name:
Andrew Stefan McCutchen

Ht: 5'10" • **Wt:** 185

Hometown/Club: Fort Meade, FL/Pittsburgh Pirates

DOB: October 10, 1986

Position: Center field

Salary: $500,000

Bats/Throws: Right/Right

Fast stat: 194: Andrew led the National League this year with 19 hits.

Did you know?: Andrew has stolen 20 or more bases in each of his major league seasons.

As a kid: Andrew was a star athlete in high school. In addition to baseball, he played football and ran on the track team.

Favorite foods/fun tidbit: Andrew hasn't gotten a haircut in five years.

Fun fact: Andrew's favorite restaurant is Brazilian steakhouse chain Texas de Brazil, since they serve unlimited meat to diners.

Fun fact: Even though he only made $500,000 in 2012, he signed a contract extension before the season that will pay him over $50 million over the next six years.

Favorite music: Andrew likes rap music, especially Lil Wayne.

Biography

One of the most exciting young players in the game today, Andrew McCutchen has put the Pirates franchise on his back and carried them to contention for the first time in more than 20 years. Though the team still has a long way to go, their rock in center field is a great foundation for the team to build upon.

A home-grown prospect from the Pittsburgh system, McCutchen earned his first call-up when the team traded starting center fielder Nate McLouth in 2009. He rewarded the team for their trust in his ability, singling in his first career at-bat. Within a week McCutchen had recorded a four-hit game and his time in the minors was over for good. Even though he missed out on more than two months of the season, the young center fielder finished his rookie year having batted .286 with 12 home runs, 54 RBI, and 22 stolen bases.

As his game matured, McCutchen quickly earned the respect of fans and opponents alike. Though many saw him as an All-Star, he was snubbed in 2010. He hit four more homers and stole 11 more bases than his rookie year and was stout in center field all year long.

The Pirates contended for most of the summer in 2011, with much of the credit going to McCutchen. Named an All-Star for the first time, the season ended in disappointment as both McCutchen and the team faded down the stretch.

He continued to improve in 2012, earning another All-Star berth based on his strong first half. McCutchen demolished several career marks, hitting .327 with 31 homers and 96 RBI at the plate and winning a Gold Glove in the field. One of the best young outfielders in the game today, McCutchen is slowly bringing the Pirates franchise back to relevancy for the first time since a young Barry Bonds patrolled the outfield.

Josh Hamilton

#32

Statistics

Full name: Joshua Holt Hamilton

Ht: 6'4" • **Wt:** 240

Hometown/Club: Raleigh, NC/ Texas Rangers

DOB: May 21, 1981

Position: Left field

Salary: $13,750,000

Bats/Throws: Left/Left

Fast stat: .359: During his MVP season in 2010, Josh hit for a league-leading .359 average.

Personal homepage: www.tripleplayministries.com

Did you know?: Josh was the first overall pick in the 1999 draft but personal problems delayed his big-league debut until 2007.

As a kid: In high school Josh was as big of a pitching prospect as he was an outfield prospect. His fastball reached the upper-90s his senior year.

Favorite foods/fun tidbit: Josh likes to start his day with a bowl of Fruity Pebbles.

Fun fact: 28: Josh hit 28 home runs in the first round of the 2008 Home Run Derby, a record for a single round.

Fun fact: Josh's charity that he founded with his wife has built an orphanage in the African country of Uganda.

Favorite music: Faith is very important to Josh, and his favorite music is Christian rock.

Biography

It took Josh Hamilton longer than it should have to reach the majors, but since he's conquered his personal demons he's become one of the best players in baseball. A five-tool prospect and a young man of excellent character, it was a no-brainer when the Tampa Bay Rays selected Hamilton first overall in 1999.

After an impressive first season in the minors, however, the wheels fell off for Hamilton. He fell into the wrong crowd while recovering from an injury and became addicted to drugs, coming nowhere close to the major leagues and spending three full seasons out of baseball completely. Hamilton looked like a bust.

He cleaned up his life, however, and returned to the game in 2007, when he made his debut with the Cincinnati Reds. His long road back earned Hamilton a standing ovation in his first at-bat, while his play earned him a regular spot starting for the Reds. He was traded to the Texas Rangers in the offseason and slotted into their center-field job immediately.

He played in a career-high 156 games that first year in Texas, proving once and for all that his recovery was no fluke. His 130 RBI also remain Hamilton's career best. Though he has been occasionally limited by injuries, when Hamilton is healthy he may be the best pure hitter in baseball. He led the Rangers to back-to-back World Series appearances, winning the MVP along the way in 2010.

This year, Hamilton had the strongest first half of his career. Though his numbers did not remain as strong as they did early, Hamilton still hit a career-high 43 homers and drove in 128 runs as the Rangers made another playoff appearance. One of the best players in the majors, Josh Hamilton has finally delivered on the potential that the Rays saw in him so many years ago.

11

Yoenis Cespedes

Statistics

Full name:
Yoenis Céspedes

Ht: 5'10" • **Wt:** 210

Hometown/Club: Campechuela, Cuba/Oakland A's

DOB: October 18, 1985

Position: Outfield

Salary: $6,500,000

Bats/Throws: Right/Right

Fast stat: .458: When Yoenis hit .458 as Cuba's starting center fielder in the 2009 World Baseball Classic, he became one of the hottest Cuban prospects in years.

Did you know?: Yoenis' mom was a star softball player and pitched for Cuba in the 2000 Olympics.

As a kid: Cespedes loved baseball as a kid and idolized Manny Ramirez. When Yoenis defected from Cuba, he fled to Manny's home country, the Dominican Republic.

Favorite foods/fun tidbit:
Even though he was a star in Cuba, Cespedes made the same salary as every other player, about $125 a month.

Fun fact: 23: Cespedes was considered a strong hitter in Cuba, but the lack of power pitchers in the country made it surprising when he hit 23 home runs in his first year facing quality pitching in the majors.

Favorite music: Yoenis loves the music of his homeland, Cuba, but also enjoys other Latin music and rap.

Biography

Perhaps the biggest prospect to come out of Cuba in the last two decades, Yoenis Cespedes—like many of his countrymen—had to take the long road to the big leagues. A star since his teen years in his native Cuba, Cespedes was known around the country as an elite center fielder. A strong showing in the 2009 World Baseball Classic proved to the world that he could hit major league pitching, but Cespedes still had to toil in the obscurity of the Cuban National Series.

After batting .333 with 33 home runs and 99 RBI in the 90-game 2011 season, Cespedes figured to be a fixture yet again for Cuba's powerful national team as they turned their attentions to international competition. When he was named to the third team, however, Cespedes decided that the time was right to finally chase his major league dream. Cespedes, his mother, and some other family escaped from the island in a speedboat, eventually reaching the Dominican Republic and freedom.

Since signing with the Oakland A's before the 2012 season, Cespedes has admitted to having trouble adjusting to the capitalist economy of the United States. He had never owned a bicycle in Cuba, let alone a car, and he found the lifestyle overwhelming.

None of that affected his play on the field. Cespedes immediately lived up to the hype. Considered a five-tool player, Cespedes took up residence in the Oakland outfield on Opening Day and recorded a double against Seattle ace Felix Hernandez in his second at-bat. He hit a homer in his second game and from there, Cespedes was rolling. He hit .292 in his first major league season, socking 23 homers and driving in 82 runs as he helped the A's to the playoffs. As he continues to become more comfortable in America, look for Cespedes to become even better in the years to come.

"The beauty of him is that he hits the ball hard to all fields."

—Nationals manager Davey Johnson

#34

Bryce Harper

Statistics

Full name: Bryce Aron Max Harper

Ht: 6'3" • **Wt:** 215

Hometown/Club: Las Vegas, NV/ Washington Nationals

DOB: October 16, 1992

Position: Center field

Salary: $500,000

Bats/Throws: Left/Right

Fast stat: 17: Bryce finished high school after his sophomore year and began to play college baseball at the age of 17.

Did you know?: Bryce wears the number 34 in honor of Mickey Mantle. The numbers add up to Mantle's jersey number, seven.

As a kid: Bryce's entire life revolved around baseball when he was a kid. He could swing a bat almost from the time he could walk.

Favorite foods/fun tidbit: Bryce's brother, Bryan, was drafted by the Nationals in 2011.

Fun fact: This year when Bryce made his major league debut, he became the youngest person to appear in the majors since 2005.

Fun fact: Bryce's 22 home runs were the most by a teenaged player in the last 45 years.

Favorite music: Bryce enjoys current rap music and also likes classic rock.

Biography

One of the most-hyped prospects in baseball, Bryce Harper arrived in the major leagues with big expectations and has fulfilled them at every turn.

Groomed from childhood to be a major leaguer, Harper's life was all about baseball from a young age. He left high school after his sophomore year, earning his GED so he could move on to college and better prepare himself for professional baseball. He went to a community college in Nevada and started at the age of 17, impressing against much older players in a wooden-bat conference. Already a big-name prospect, his 31 homers in 66 games made him the most highly touted amateur player in years.

It was a no-brainer when the Washington Nationals selected him first overall, putting Harper into a system that also included pitching phenom Stephen Strasburg. Though Harper was initially a catcher, he was moved to the outfield in an effort to speed up his development.

After a strong spring in 2012, Harper began the season with Class AAA Syracuse. He did not stay there long, as an injury to Ryan Zimmerman saw Harper reach the majors before the end of April. He had a double and drove in a run in his first game, a promising start for a prospect with so much attention focused on him. Harper's first full month was full of successes and milestones, including his first big-league homer and a steal of home that proved to be a popular highlight across the country. Named the Rookie of the Month for May, the teenager's career was off to a bright start.

Harper was named to the All-Star Game as a replacement for Giancarlo Stanton, and though he cooled off after the break, Harper still enjoyed a strong summer. He found his sweet swing again in September, hitting .330 for the month and helping the Nationals to the playoffs. Though he hit a homer in Game 5 of the Division Series against the Cardinals, the Nationals were eliminated. Still, it was a massively successful season for one of the brightest prospects baseball has seen in years.

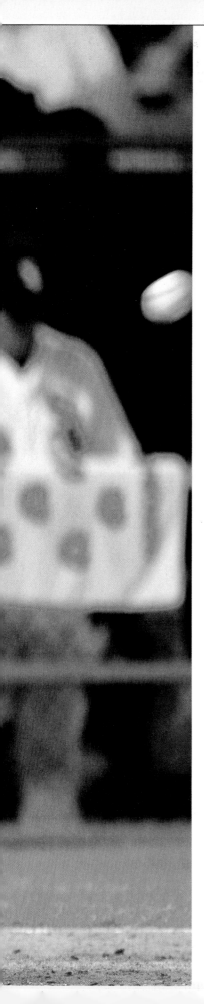

> *"I believe Albert's the best, just because of the way he plays the game."*
> —former Cardinals manager Tony La Russa

Albert Pujols

Statistics

Full name:
José Alberto Pujols

Ht: 6'3" • **Wt:** 210

Hometown/Club: Santo Domingo, Dominican Republic/Los Angeles Angels of Anaheim

DOB: January 16, 1980

Position: First base

Salary: $12,000,000

Bats/Throws: Right/Right

Fast stat: 3: Albert has won the National League MVP award three times in his career.

Personal homepage:
www.pujolsfamilyfoundation.org

Did you know?: Albert has the highest career batting average among all active players, hitting for a .325 average.

As a kid: Albert was raised mainly by his grandmother and played baseball using limes for balls and a milk carton as his glove. He moved to New York when he was 16.

Favorite foods/fun tidbit:
In the first game of his only college season, Albert hit a grand slam and turned an unassisted triple play.

Fun fact: Albert is the only player in baseball history to hit at least .300 with 30 homers and 100 RBI in each of his first 10 seasons.

Favorite music: Albert enjoys Christian rap music, especially artists from the St. Louis area, since he played there for so long.

Biography

One of the best hitters to ever play the game, Albert Pujols is one of the biggest stars in baseball. His old-school approach to hitting has won him fans and admirers at every turn, while his dedication to charity has made him a shining example of how athletes can use their platform as celebrities to help others.

Considered a throw-back to old time baseball players, Pujols is truly a student of the game. He approaches hitting as a science, and that attitude has made him into one of the best in the history of the sport. No other player has hit .300 while belting 30 homers and driving in 100 runs for 10 straight seasons to start his career, and Pujols did so with ease. The three-time MVP has made nine All-Star appearances and won a pair of World Series, making him one of the most decorated active players, along with Derek Jeter.

This native of the Dominican Republic moved to the United States as a teenager to chase his baseball dream, and he has delivered on his promise in a big way. He was named the Rookie of the Year unanimously after driving in 130 runs in 2001, a sign of things to come. The then-outfielder hit 34 home runs in 2002, driving in 127 runs and proving that he was no fluke.

St. Louis reached the World Series in 2004 on the back of their superstar and though they fell short, the team earned valuable experience. They were back in 2006, with a Pujols homer off of Justin Verlander in Game 1 setting the tone for the Series. The Cardinals won the championship and Pujols won his first Gold Glove for his efforts that year.

Another world championship followed in 2011, and though Pujols has remained one of the best players in the game, baseball is not everything in his life. Pujols has started a charity to help people with Down syndrome as well as the poor of the Dominican Republic, and he is frequently seen helping others on off days and during the offseason.

"He looks like The Natural."
—Brewers radio broadcaster Jim Powell

#8

Ryan Braun

Statistics

Full name: Ryan Joseph Braun

Ht: 6'1" • **Wt:** 190

Hometown/Club: Los Angeles, CA/Milwaukee Brewers

DOB: November 17, 1983

Position: Left field

Salary: $6,000,000

Bats/Throws: Right/Right

Fast stat: 5: Braun is the only player in franchise history to drive in 100 runs in five consecutive years.

Did you know?: Braun reached 1,000 hits faster than Pete Rose, baseball's all-time hit king.

As a kid: Braun was a straight-A student in high school, earning just one B in four years.

Favorite foods/fun tidbit: Braun has the third best slugging percentage of any active player, behind only Albert Pujols and Alex Rodriguez

Fun fact: 41: Braun led the National League with 41 homers in 2012.

Fun fact: Braun is one of only nine players in history to have a season with 40 homers and 30 stolen bases.

Favorite music:
Ryan enjoys hip-hop.

Biography

The best young slugger in the game, Ryan Braun is bashing homers at a pace that may put him among the all-time leaders by the time he retires. The National League MVP in 2011, Braun is one of the most devastating offensive weapons in baseball and led the league in homers in 2012.

Braun stormed onto the scene after being called up to the majors for the first time in May 2007. He recorded 21 RBI in his first full month in the big leagues, proving immediately that he could hit major league pitching. Braun won the National League's Rookie of the Year honors and led the Brewers in batting average and slugging percentage.

He has been an All-Star every year since, terrorizing National League pitchers with his bat. Braun enjoys considerable success against left-handers, speculating that he is best against lefties because his dad is left handed and pitched to him so often as a youth. Continuing his unprecedented hot streak to start his career, Braun continued to hit well in 2008, eventually recording 134 runs over his first 162 career games. Braun started for the National League in the All-Star Game and the Brewers reached the playoffs for the first time since 1982.

The next year, Braun led the National League in hits, proving that power is just one element of his game. In 2011, Braun lifted the Brewers to a Central Division championship after hitting 33 home runs and driving in 111 runs. He bettered those numbers in 2012, socking a career-high 41 homers and driving in 112 runs. Though a bit of controversy marred the first part of Braun's 2012, he cleared his name and went on to continue to show that the best hitter in the big leagues just might be the Brewers' left fielder.

"Jimmy Rollins is a great man to us, as a brother, as a father, as a caretaker."

—Odong Henry, the coach of the Ugandan Little League team that Rollins mentors.

Jimmy Rollins

Statistics

Full name: James Calvin Rollins

Ht: 5'8" • **Wt:** 170

Hometown/Club: Oakland, CA/ Philadelphia Phillies

DOB: November 27, 1978

Position: Shortstop

Salary: $11,000,000

Bats/Throws: Switch/Right

Fast stat: 46: Hyped as a speedster, Rollins lived up to expectations as a rookie by leading the National League with 46 stolen bases in 2001.

Personal homepage: www.jimmyrollins.com

Did you know?: Rollins once hit safely in 38 straight games, setting a franchise record.

As a kid: Jimmy enjoyed watching his mom play softball and credits her with helping to develop his mental approach to the game.

Favorite foods/fun tidbit: Rollins spent two weeks in 2011 in the African nation of Uganda, working with young baseball players trying to improve their lives through sports. The team qualified for the Little League World Series but could not attend.

Fun fact: Rollins had the best fielding percentage among all shortstops in 2012. He won his fourth Gold Glove for his efforts.

Favorite music: Jimmy enjoys hip-hop and owns his own record label.

Biography

Sparkplug Jimmy Rollins is one of the smallest players in the major leagues, but his success has proven that a player does not need to be big in order to be larger than life in baseball. Seen mostly as a speedster early in his career, Rollins has added power to his game in recent years and rounded into a true five-tool player. The former MVP is one of the most popular players in the game and always seems to deliver in big moments.

After impressing in a late-season call-up in 2000, there was much hype surrounding Rollins as he began his first full major league season in 2001. The young player delivered, leading the league with 46 stolen bases and earning All-Star honors. The next year Rollins became the first shortstop in major league history to earn selections to the All-Star Game in each of his first two years.

Rollins continued to improve his offensive numbers as he grew into his slight frame, adding as much muscle as he could support while still running the bases effectively. He was again an All-Star in 2005 and finished the year by hitting safely in the last 36 games of the season. He set the franchise record for homers by a shortstop the next year, belting 25.

In 2007 Rollins came to spring training as a man on a mission. He saw the Phillies as the team to beat in the National League and set out to prove it. Rollins joined the 30-30 club by hitting more than 30 homers and stealing more than 30 bases, winning the National League's Most Valuable Player Award in one of the closest votes in history. Though the Phillies fell short of the World Series in the playoffs, they were back in 2008 and claimed the championship.

He has continued to be one of the most popular players in the major leagues and is actively involved in charity work. In 2012, Rollins recorded his 2000th career hit.

#37

> *"He's a cornerstone of this organization, and we want him to pitch for the next 10 years."*
> —teammate Drew Storen

Stephen Strasburg

Statistics

Full name:
Stephen James Strasburg

Ht: 6'4" · **Wt:** 220

Hometown/Club: San Diego, CA/ Washington Nationals

DOB: July 20, 1988

Position: Pitcher

Salary: $3,000,000

Bats/Throws: Right/Right

Fast stat: 14: Stephen struck out 14 batters in his major league debut, setting a franchise record.

Personal homepage:
www.strasburg5k.com

Did you know?: Stephen's 2012 season ended at 15 wins when he reached an innings limit placed on him before the season by the team. When the Nationals made the playoffs, they continued to rest Strasburg for 2013.

As a kid: Stephen played baseball in high school but struggled at times, including a 1–10 record as a junior.

Favorite foods/fun tidbit: Stephen pitched in the Olympics in 2008, going 1–1 and helping the United States win the bronze medal.

Fun fact: If his career ended today, Strasburg would have the second best strikeout rate of all time.

Fun fact: No pitcher struck out 100 batters in 2012 in a shorter amount of time than Strasburg.

Favorite music: Stephen likes country music, especially the Zac Brown Band.

Biography

One of the most-hyped pitching prospects in decades, Stephen Strasburg has the weight of an entire organization on his shoulders. The young Washington Nationals fireballer balances his talent with his work ethic as he attempts to become the game's next great ace.

Strasburg first became a prospect while playing for Hall of Famer Tony Gwynn at San Diego State University. Though he battled with his weight early in his college career, Strasburg disciplined himself and became a better pitcher every day, quickly turning himself into a big-name prospect. His status was solidified when he became the only college player named to the 2008 United States Olympic team that took the bronze in Beijing.

Selected first overall in the 2009 draft, Strasburg was fast-tracked through the Nationals system. Considered the biggest prospect in baseball, national media followed Strasburg everywhere he went in the minors. He earned his first call-up in June 2010 and set the baseball world on fire in his debut. Strasburg struck out 14 over seven innings, walking no one and earning the win. The hype matched the ability.

Strasburg's rookie season was unfortunately cut short in August, however, after just 12 starts. He needed Tommy John surgery on his elbow and was projected to be out for at least a year. Still, he had proven that he had the skills to be an ace in the majors.

After returning from his injury in 2011, Strasburg was ready to hit the ground running in 2012. Though his season was cut short by an innings limit imposed by the team, the young hurler still won 15 games for the best team in baseball. Strasburg was named to his first All-Star team and it has become clear that he will be an ace in the majors for years to come.

23

"He does things the right way, and that's bigger than anything else. He has everyone's respect, and that carries a lot of weight."

—White Sox manager Robin Ventura

Paul Konerko

Statistics

Full name: Paul Henry Konerko

Ht: 6'2" • **Wt:** 220

Hometown/Club: Providence, RI/ Chicago White Sox

DOB: March 5, 1976

Position: First base

Salary: $12,000,000

Bats/Throws: Right/Right

Fast stat: 2: Only two White Sox have hit 400 career homers. In addition to Konerko, Frank Thomas also reached the mark.

Did you know?: Paul was briefly considered for the White Sox's manager job in 2011. Had he been hired, Konerko would have been the first player-manager in baseball since 1986.

As a kid: When he was in high school, Paul was rated as the best catcher in the country.

Favorite foods/fun tidbit: In April 2009, Konerko and Jermaine Dye hit back-to-back home runs that marked the 300th of each man's career. It is the only time two players have hit milestone home runs in the same game.

Fun fact: Paul caught the final out in each round of the playoffs when the White Sox cruised through the playoffs to win the 2005 World Series.

Fun fact: Paul has made the All-Star Game each of the last three years, the longest streak of his career.

Favorite music: Paul enjoys hard rock and heavy metal.

Biography

Paul Konerko might be the most underrated player in the game today. Toiling for most of his career with the Chicago White Sox—the second most popular team in their own city—Konerko has quietly put up a career that may earn him consideration for the Hall of Fame. One of the most consistent sluggers in the majors, the player affectionately known as "Paulie" is a hard-working, hard-hitting team leader.

After arriving in Chicago in a trade for Mike Cameron, Konerko quickly established himself as a hard hitter and a hard worker, traits loved by the tough, blue-collar fan base of the White Sox. He quickly endeared himself to the South Side, who viewed him as a worthy heir to two-time MVP Frank Thomas at first base. The White Sox grew into contenders, making a playoff appearance in Konerko's second year with the team.

In 2005 the Sox had a year to remember. With a slugging middle of the order and colorful manager Ozzie Guillen, the White Sox used grit and hard play—trademarks of Konerko's game— to record the American League's best record. Konerko came into his own in the playoffs, carrying the White Sox in the ALCS as they moved to their first World Series since 1959. Konerko hit a grand slam in Game 2 of the World Series and helped lift the White Sox to their first championship since 1917.

Though he is little-known outside of Chicago, Konerko is one of the most popular athletes in the city. A leader on and off the diamond, he is beloved and trusted by his teammates. Konerko has recorded more than 400 career homers and has a real shot to hit 500 in his career. A six-time All-Star, including the last three years, "Paulie" still has plenty left in the tank for one more World Series run.

#28

Buster Posey

Statistics

Full name:
Gerald Dempsey Posey III

Ht: 6'1" • **Wt:** 218

Hometown/Club: Leesburg, GA/ San Francisco Giants

DOB: March 27, 1987

Position: Catcher/First base

Salary: $615,000

Bats/Throws: Right/Right

Fast stat: .336: Buster led the National League in 2012 with a .336 batting average.

Did you know?: When Buster won Rookie of the Year honors in 2010, he did so in a shortened season. He spent the first two months of the year in the minors.

As a kid: Buster's nickname actually comes from his dad, who was also called Buster as a kid.

Favorite foods/fun tidbit: Shortstop is Buster's natural position. He switched to catcher in college because his team needed him to.

Fun fact: Buster has played two full major league seasons, and both have ended with him catching the third strike of a World Series win for the Giants.

Fun fact: Buster was named the 2012 National League Comeback Player of the Year for his dramatic recovery from a career-threatening leg injury he suffered in 2011.

Favorite music: Buster enjoys country music and some rap.

Biography

An elite catcher and team leader when he's healthy, the young Buster Posey has not had an easy go of it in his short career. After a breakout rookie season, his career nearly ended on a freak play in 2011. He lost nearly an entire year to injury but has managed to bounce back in a big way in 2012. Just like his stellar rookie year, this season ended with a triumphant Posey catching the final strike of the World Series.

Called up to the majors two months into the 2010 season, Posey quickly proved that he belonged in the big leagues. Playing at first base, his season debut saw him record three hits and knock in three runs, forcing his way into Bruce Bochy's lineup with his play. Posey's talent at the dish made Bengie Molina expendable, and by the end of the month Posey was settled as the Giants new starting catcher.

The National League Rookie of the Year, despite appearing in just 108 games, Posey took less than a year to establish himself as one of the game's best catchers. He hit 18 homers and drove in 67 runs but was at his best in the playoffs. He batted .300 in the World Series, earning a championship in his first full season.

Posey started off strong in 2011, looking like his year was going to be even better than his rookie campaign. It was cut short after just 45 games, however, when the Florida Marlins' Scott Cousins collided with Posey at the plate, breaking Posey's leg and tearing ligaments in his ankle. The injury was deemed potentially career-threatening, knocking Posey out for the rest of the year.

He returned with a vengeance in 2012, immediately proving that he is suffering no long-term effects from the injury. Posey hit for a .336 average in the regular season, leading the National League, and he also earned a spot in the All-Star Game. Once again, he was excellent in the playoffs, putting an exclamation point on his recovery as he hit a two-run homer in the decisive Game 4 of the World Series.

"I've never seen anything like this. Never. I've seen some dominant pitching, but nothing like what he's going through right now."

—Mets manager Terry Collins

R.A. Dickey

Statistics

Full name: Robert Allen Dickey

Ht: 6'2" • **Wt:** 222

Hometown/Club: Nashville, TN/ New York Mets

DOB: October 29, 1974

Position: Pitcher

Salary: $4,250,000

Bats/Throws: Right/Right

Fast stat: 230: R.A. led the National League in strikeouts with 230 in 2012 despite rarely throwing a ball more than 85 miles per hour.

Did you know?: R.A. is the only active pitcher that uses the knuckleball as his primary pitch.

As a kid: R.A. excelled in the classroom as well as on the diamond. He attended a very prestigious high school in Nashville and was later named an academic All-American at Tennessee.

Favorite foods/fun tidbit: During the 2011 offseason, R.A. went to Africa and climbed the famous Mount Kilimanjaro.

Fun fact: R.A.'s 20 wins this season beat his previous career high by nine.

Fun fact: In June, R.A. threw back-to-back one-hitters, the first time a National League pitcher had accomplished the feat since 1944.

Favorite book: R.A. is an avid reader and names his bats after his favorite book characters.

Biography

The unassuming R.A. Dickey was just trying to hold on to his major league career as 2012 began. A borderline major leaguer in the first years of his career, Dickey had trouble staying on a major league roster until he switched to the knuckleball. The slow, unpredictable pitch saved his career but the results—heading into 2012, at least—had been modest. An 11-win season in 2010 was a career best for the aging right hander, but almost no one saw his dominant 2012 coming.

A conventional pitcher when he first came up with the Texas Rangers in 2001, his stuff was nothing special as he bounced through the majors and minors for the next several years. He did, however, own a devastating forkball that he later learned was actually a form of knuckleball. Dickey set about perfecting the pitch, and though it kept him on major league rosters every year, the results were unspectacular.

One of the most surprising sports stories of 2012, Dickey came into the year with low expectations after going 8–13 the previous year. Though he'd made a career high in starts and thrown over 200 innings for the first time, the aging knuckleballer was seen as little more than a back of the rotation pitcher.

What happened next was nothing short of remarkable. Dickey went off on a hot streak in the first half of 2012 that could match up against player in history. Dickey began to record strikeouts at a furious pace, setting team records previously held by Pedro Martinez, who could throw nearly 15 miles per hour harder than Dickey. He threw back-to-back one-hitters in June, missing out on a no-hit bid when David Wright had trouble handling a ball.

Dickey's dominant first half (he was 5–0 in June alone) earned him his first All-Star appearance. The wins kept coming in the second half, as he put up a Cy Young–caliber season at the age of 38. His 20 wins, 230 strikeouts, five complete games, and 2.73 ERA all blew away his previous career highs.

> *"You don't see many guys with that mix of power and average. Some of those guys only hit home runs, but he can hit .300."*
> —fellow All-Star Corey Hart

#19

Joey Votto

Statistics

Full name: Joseph Daniel Votto

Ht: 6'3" • **Wt:** 225

Hometown/Club: Toronto, ON/Cincinnati Reds

DOB: September 10, 1983

Position: First base

Salary: $9,500,000

Bats/Throws: Left/Right

Fast stat: 3: Canadians who have won MVP awards. Larry Walker and Justin Morneau are the others.

Did you know?: Joey hit his first major league home run in his second career at-bat.

As a kid: In addition to baseball, Joey was excellent at hockey and basketball.

Favorite foods/fun tidbit: One of Joey's favorite sports memories was watching Joe Carter hit a walk-off home run to win the 1993 World Series for the Toronto Blue Jays.

Fun fact: To make himself look better for scouts combing through Canada, Joey used a wooden bat in high school.

Fun fact: Joey has the longest contract in baseball. He is signed through the 2024 season.

Favorite music: Joey enjoys classic rock.

Biography

The smashing success of Joey Votto in Cincinnati has proven a few things. The first is that a player does not need to be in a large market to be a superstar; given Votto's numbers and salary, he certainly qualifies. The second is that major league scouts need to spend more time combing the high school fields of Canada, as the nation has provided two MVPs in recent years, with Justin Morneau also claiming top honors in the last few years.

Drafted straight out of high school, it took Votto a few years to adjust to the professional game after playing against less-skilled competition in Canada. He became a student of the game, carrying with him a copy of a book about hitting written by his favorite player, Ted Williams. His hard work paid off, earning Votto a call-up in September 2007. Votto hit a home run in his second major league at-bat and hit .321 in limited action, earning him a spot on the Opening Day roster in 2008.

No rookie hit for a better average or hit more homers than Votto in 2008, though he fell short in Rookie of the Year voting. Still, he was already seen as a future star in the game. After hitting .322 and socking 25 homers in 2009, it was clear that Votto was one of the best hitting first basemen in the game.

He truly broke out in 2010, starting off the year with a bang by recording three hits—including a homer—on Opening Day. Votto threw the team on his shoulders and carried them to the postseason thanks to a .324 season where he hit 37 homers and drove in 113 runs, earning him MVP honors. He missed a unanimous win by a single vote. Votto has continued to play like an MVP for the last two years, though injuries limited him to 111 games in 2012.

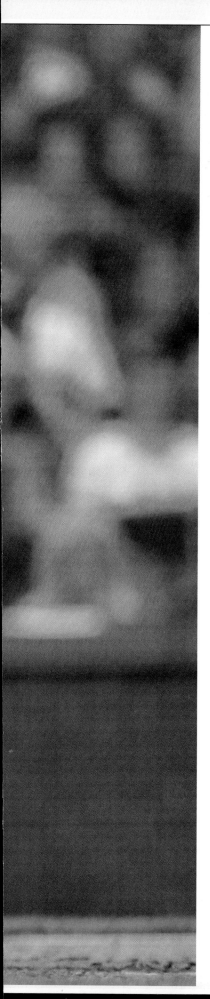

> **"He looks like he's going to hit the ball hard every time up there."**
> —Hall of Famer George Brett

Carlos Beltran

Statistics

Full name: Carlos Iván Beltrán

Ht: 6'1" • **Wt:** 215

Hometown/Club: Manati, Puerto Rico/St. Louis Cardinals

DOB: April 24, 1977

Position: Outfield

Salary: $13,000,000

Bats/Throws: Switch/Right

Fast stat: 2,000: Carlos reached the 2,000-hit milestone in 2012.

Did you know?: Carlos is the only switch hitter in major league history to hit 300 home runs and steal 300 bases.

As a kid: One of Carlos' best memories in baseball was winning a national championship as a 10-year-old in Puerto Rico.

Favorite foods/fun tidbit: Carlos saved a part of his salary every year in an attempt to establish a high school. Today, the Carlos Beltran Baseball Academy helps young Puerto Ricans try to achieve their big-league dreams.

Fun fact: Beltran did not start his career as a switch hitter. When he arrived at spring training for his second professional season, he thought that hitting from the left side looked like fun so he gave it a shot.

Fun fact: 11: Carlos has never been caught stealing in the playoffs. His 11 stolen bases without recording an out are a major league postseason record.

Favorite music: Carlos enjoys Latin pop music.

Biography

One of the most consistent players in the game today, Carlos Beltran arrived in the major leagues nearly 15 years ago, hyped as one of the game's next great outfielders. A few trades later, Beltran is still bashing homers and leading his teams to success, posting some of the best numbers in baseball over the last decade.

One of the best postseason hitters of his generation, Beltran has never shied away from big situations. Among other records, his OPS (on-base plus slugging) in the playoffs is better than the career marks for both Babe Ruth and Lou Gehrig—some lofty company. He has never been caught stealing in the playoffs.

Beltran was a highly touted prospect coming up in the Kansas City Royals system, reaching the big leagues in center field flanked by fellow hot prospects Johnny Damon and Jermaine Dye. Though all three saw their greatest successes elsewhere, the young trio made up the most exciting young outfield in baseball at the time. Beltran won Rookie of the Year honors in 1999, socking 22 homers and driving in 108 runs.

After several seasons of hitting more than 20 homers and driving in 100 runs but playing for uncompetitive Kansas City teams, he was shipped off to the Houston Astros. Though the team fell short in the NLCS, Beltran tied a major league record with eight homers in the postseason.

From there it was off to the New York Mets as a free agent. An All-Star his first two years with the team, Beltran socked 41 home runs in 2006 and led the Mets to the NLCS. Though the team fell short of the World Series, another three homers boosted Beltran's career total to 11 homers in 22 postseason games. He also won the first of three consecutive Gold Gloves that year.

The first switch hitter to reach 300 homers and 300 stolen bases, Beltran has been a unique weapon throughout his career. Though his Cardinals fell just short of the World Series in 2012, Beltran was again solid in the playoffs. His long-awaited World Series berth may be just around the corner in 2013.

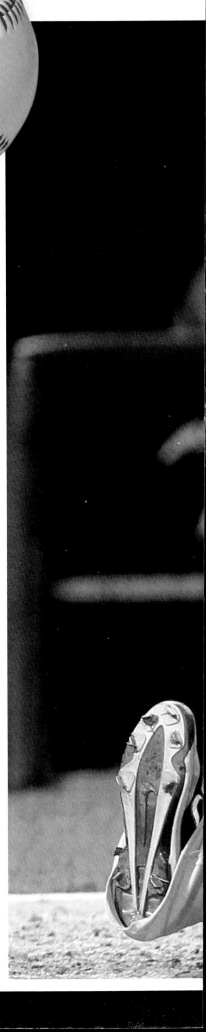

> *"He makes it look easy. He's amazing. I've never seen anybody hitting like that."*
> —former teammate Francisco Liriano

#7

Joe Mauer

Statistics

Full name: Joseph Patrick Mauer

Ht: 6'5" • **Wt:** 220

Hometown/Club: St. Paul, MN/ Minnesota Twins

DOB: April 19, 1983

Position: Catcher/First base

Salary: $23,000,000

Bats/Throws: Left/Right

Fast stat: 3: Joe has won three batting titles, the most by a catcher in baseball history.

Did you know?: Mauer is the only athlete to ever be named USA Today High School Player of the Year in two sports.

As a kid: Joe was very popular in his home city of St. Paul, with him mom joking that since the family was friends with or related to everyone in the city, she always knew when Joe was up to something.

Favorite foods/fun tidbit: Joe's brother, Jake, is a former Twins minor leaguer and is currently the manager of one of the team's minor league affiliates.

Fun fact: During the 2006 season, Joe and teammate Justin Morneau shared a house and made it into their "bachelor pad."

Fun fact: $184 million: Joe's contract is worth $184 million, the richest contract for a catcher in the history of baseball.

Favorite music: Joe likes all kinds of music, but is a big rap fan. He has a home studio and records his own music.

Biography

Hometown hero Joe Mauer never had to leave the Twin Cities to become a superstar. Perhaps the best catcher of his generation, the tough, hard-hitting player from St. Paul is one of the most popular players in the game.

The national player of the year in both football and baseball as a high school senior, Mauer could have played either sport at a high level. He was also a two-time All-State player in basketball, averaging more than 20 points per game. After turning down a football scholarship to Florida State, Mauer's hometown Twins made him the first overall pick in the 2001 draft.

Mauer was one of the best young catchers in baseball as he got his feet wet in 2004 and 2005 before he broke out in 2006. That year, Mauer became the first catcher in history to lead the major leagues in batting average as he hit .347. It was the first of an unprecedented three American League batting titles for Mauer and he remains the only catcher in AL history to lead the circuit in batting average.

He continued to hit at a record pace and draw fans throughout the country with his style when playing the game, which included a set of throwback sideburns that would not have been out of place in the 1970s. Mauer's defense continued to improve, as he won his first Gold Glove in 2008 while also leading the American League in batting average.

Mauer led the league in average and several other offensive categories in 2009, with his .365 average sitting as the best mark by a catcher in major league history. The highest paid catcher in the history of the game, Mauer was again an All-Star in 2012 as he began to play more at first base, a move aimed at keeping him a star in the Twin Cities for years to come.

> *"I have the greatest job in the world. Only one person can have it. You have shortstops on other teams—I'm not knocking other teams—but there's only one shortstop on the Yankees."* —Derek Jeter

Derek Jeter

Statistics

Full name: Derek Sanderson Jeter

Ht: 6'3" • **Wt:** 175

Hometown/Club: Kalamazoo, MI/ New York Yankees

DOB: June 26, 1974

Position: Shortstop

Salary: $16,000,000

Bats/Throws: Right/Right

Fast stat: 3,304: No player in the storied history of the Yankees has as many hits for the team as Jeter's 3,304.

Personal homepage: www.derekjeter.com

Did you know?: No player has played in more games for the Yankees than Jeter.

As a kid: Derek was born in New Jersey but raised in Michigan. During the summer he would visit his grandparents back in New Jersey and go to Yankee games with them, becoming a fan of the team.

Favorite foods/fun tidbit: Yankees scouts were so high on Jeter during his draft year that they were already predicting that he would become a Hall of Fame–caliber player.

Fun fact: Derek led the American League in hits in 2012 with 216. It was the first time he led the league in hits since 1999.

Favorite music: Derek likes to listen to R&B and one of his favorite singers is Alicia Keys.

Biography

One of the best to ever play the game, Derek Jeter is among the most beloved players in baseball history. The face of the Yankees, the shortstop has been living his childhood dream for more than 15 years and is a sure-fire Hall of Famer. Still playing at an elite level long after many pundits had written him off as washed up, Jeter continues to surprise with his ability, even in the twilight of his career.

Bursting onto the scene in 1996 in his first full season in the big leagues, Jeter announced his arrival to the baseball world by hitting a homer on Opening Day. He was a unanimous choice for Rookie of the Year that season, leading the Yankees to a World Series championship. Jeter put the team on his shoulders in the postseason when some of the team's big names struggled, making him an instant superstar in New York.

Jeter only got better as his career began to blossom with the Yankees. The team won three more World Series titles in the next four years, with Jeter becoming the centerpiece of the organization. A tremendously talented player with an easy smile and no skeletons in his closet, the New York and national media made him one of the biggest names in baseball, even as homers were flying out of ballparks at a record pace in places like St. Louis and Chicago.

Since 1998 Jeter has only missed being named to the All-Star Game twice, earning 13 selections. A five-time Gold Glover, Jeter's defense remains as stout as ever, with an image of him jumping toward third base as he fires to first becoming the signature symbol of his game. With five World Series wins under his belt and a slew of Yankee records to his name, there is no doubt that Jeter will be a first-ballot Hall of Famer when his career is over.

"No one gets anywhere by themselves. I count my blessings. I know where I want to go, but I'll never forget where I came from."

—Adam Jones

Adam Jones

Statistics

Full name: Adam La Marque Jones

Ht: 6'3" • **Wt:** 225

Hometown/Club: San Diego, CA/ Baltimore Orioles

DOB: August 1, 1985

Position: Center field

Salary: $6,150,000

Bats/Throws: Right/Right

Fast stat: 32: Jones' 32 home runs in 2012 were a career high.

Did you know?: Both times that Adam has made the All-Star team, he's won the Gold Glove in the same year.

As a kid: Adam's best sports growing up were football and basketball. He didn't swing a baseball bat until he was 12.

Favorite foods/fun tidbit: Using Twitter, Adam occasionally asks Oriole fans how he should wear his uniform for games.

Fun fact: 162: Adam played in all 162 games for the first time in his career in 2012.

Fun fact: It took Adam until his 13th at-bat in the major leagues to get his first hit.

Favorite music: Adam likes rap music, including Jay-Z, Dr. Dre, and Tupac.

Biography

Making the playoffs in 2012 was a sweet redemption for Adam Jones. Raised in poverty, overlooked in his first major league stop in Seattle, and seemingly forgotten by the national media in Baltimore, taking the national stage as the leader of one of baseball's best teams has left Jones smiling and hungry for more.

A part of a huge trade that brought Erik Bedard to Seattle, Jones was just a cog in the wheel as he arrived in Baltimore. He was a good prospect but had scuffled in his stints in the majors over the last two years, struggling to get his feet wet with irregular playing time. He broke out upon his arrival in Baltimore in 2008, quickly establishing himself as a centerpiece for the team's future. Jones hit .270 and drove in 57 runs in his first full major league season, leaving him eager for more in 2009.

Jones came out of the gate flying in 2009, earning an All-Star nod for his efforts in the first half of the season. He starred in the game, driving in the winning run in the American League's 4-3 win. Adam Jones was quickly becoming a star.

After almost exactly matching his 2009 numbers in 2010, Jones took another step forward in 2011. He belted a career-high 25 home runs, further establishing himself as the best player on the Orioles. As 2012 began, he was eager to take his place among the game's elite outfielders.

Jones carried his team as they pushed their way to a playoff berth in 2012. Playing in all 162 games, the dynamic outfielder set another career-high with 32 homers and also stole 16 bases, proving that he is a multi-dimensional weapon. A bright spot for one of baseball's most exciting young teams, Jones will certainly be a player to watch in the years to come.

39

#14

David Price

Statistics

Full name: David Taylor Price

Ht: 6'6" · **Wt:** 220

Hometown/Club: Murfreesboro, TN/Tampa Bay Rays

DOB: August 26, 1985

Position: Pitcher

Salary: $4,350,000

Bats/Throws: Left/Left

Fast stat: $5.6 million: When Price was drafted first overall in 2007, he was given what was—at the time—the second largest rookie signing bonus in baseball history.

Did you know?: The first hit that Price gave up in the majors was a home run to Derek Jeter.

As a kid: David once nearly quit baseball to go and work at a fast food restaurant.

Favorite foods/fun tidbit: David loves to eat bacon, and his French bulldog named Astro is also a fan.

Fun fact: David is well-known for his fast pace on the mound, generally taking only five to seven seconds to pitch after he gets the ball from the catcher.

Fun fact: Pitching out of the bullpen in the 2008 playoffs, Price's save in Game 7 of the ALCS sent the Rays to the World Series for the first time.

Favorite music: David enjoys rap and electronic music.

Biography

Tampa Bay Rays pitcher David Price is one of the most feared in baseball. A steady performer with lots of big-game experience, Price shies away from no hitter. The first overall draft pick in 2007, it took little more than a year before Price got the call to the big leagues in September 2008.

The surprising Rays worked their way into the playoffs that year and slotted the young hurler in their bullpen, with the hard-throwing lefty giving Joe Maddon a dynamic weapon to use late in games. He came through with a memorable save in Game 7 of the ALCS, helping to knock out the defending champion Boston Red Sox and sending the Rays to the World Series for the first time. Though the Rays fell short of winning it all, Price picked up another save in Game 2 against the Philadelphia Phillies.

With so much early experience, Price immediately became wise beyond his years as he transitioned into a full-time starter. He made 23 starts in his first full season in 2009, going 10–7 and striking out 102 batters.

Ready to break out in 2010, Price came roaring out of the gates and won 10 games before any other American League pitcher. Named the starting pitcher for the American League in the All-Star Game, Price eventually finished the year second in the league with 19 wins.

Price has continued to pitch at an All-Star level for the last two years, including a 20-win campaign in 2012. He is the youngest pitcher to win 20 in the American League since 2004 and the only one to reach the mark with the Rays. Perhaps the best young pitcher in the game right now, Price is a devastating weapon that gives his team a great chance to win every time he toes the rubber.

> *"He's the best I've ever seen in right field going back on a baseball."*
> —Braves catcher David Ross

#22

Jason Heyward

Statistics

Full name: Jason Alias Heyward

Ht: 6'5" • **Wt:** 240

Hometown/Club: Ridgewood, NJ/ Atlanta Braves

DOB: August 9, 1989

Position: Right field

Salary: $565,000

Bats/Throws: Left/Left

Fast stat: 471: Feet Heyward's first career home run flew.

Did you know?: Jason homered in his first major league at-bat.

As a kid: Despite spending nearly all of his childhood in the Atlanta suburbs, Jason still cheered for the Yankees and Mets.

Favorite foods/fun tidbit: In his 2010 All-Star season, Jason became the first Braves player in over 10 years to steal home.

Fun fact: Jason wears No. 22 in honor of a high school teammate and close friend.

Fun fact: 2012 is Jason's first Gold Glove–winning year.

Favorite music: Jason enjoys rap music, especially Outkast.

Biography

After hitting a home run in his first major league at-bat, it was impossible to ignore the talents of Jason Heyward. The young slugger had the size and look of someone ready to bash home runs for decades to come and was a speedster on the basepaths. With all of the tools necessary to become a star, it was clear from the start that Heyward was going to be something big.

Considered the best prospect in baseball when he was called up, Heyward delivered on his promise from the start. Named the Rookie of the Month for each of his first two months in the big leagues, Heyward was driving in runs and tracking down just about every ball hit his way. Named to the All-Star Game, Heyward unfortunately had to miss out due to injury. He finished his rookie year with 18 homers and finished second to Buster Posey in Rookie of the Year voting.

In 2011, Heyward started the year just like he had begun the previous campaign, hitting a homer in his first at-bat of the year. This year, Heyward displayed the best range of any right fielder in baseball, winning the Gold Glove for his efforts. He also hit a career-high 27 home runs while driving in 82. As Heyward comes into his own as a major leaguer, there is little doubt that he will be one of the most dynamic players in the game for at least a decade to come. A combination of speed, power, and elite defense, Heyward truly has it all.

> *"He's bulletproof, as far as I'm concerned. Whether there's a lefthander on the mound or a righthander on the mound, he beats us up pretty good."*
> —former Yankees manager Joe Torre

#34

David Ortiz

Statistics

Full name:
David Américo Ortiz

Ht: 6'4" • **Wt:** 250

Hometown/Club: Santo Domingo, Dominican Republic/ Boston Red Sox

DOB: November 18, 1975

Position:
Designated hitter/first base

Salary: $14,580,000

Bats/Throws: Left/Left

Fast stat: 54: Ortiz holds the Red Sox single-season home run record after he belted 54 homers in 2006.

Personal homepage:
www.davidortiz.com

Did you know?: David is considered the best clutch hitter in Red Sox history.

As a kid: David's easy smile was his trademark growing up in the Dominican Republic. The oldest of four kids, he was easygoing and known in his family for his sense of humor.

Favorite foods/fun tidbit: David's wife is from Wisconsin and he has become an avid fan of the Green Bay Packers over the years.

Fun fact: David has made eight All-Star teams in his career, including three straight through 2012.

Favorite music: David enjoys reggaeton music and has recorded songs and made music videos.

Biography

The man affectionately known as "Big Papi" is one of the best clutch hitters in baseball history. A rotund slugger with an easy smile and a playfulness that suggests a true love for the game, David Ortiz is one of the most popular players in baseball for good reason. One of the best hitters of his generation, Ortiz has always been there in big moments for his Boston Red Sox, bashing many memorable home runs as the team gained a place among the game's elite with two World Series titles in four years.

An eight-time All-Star, Ortiz began his career with the Minnesota Twins. Though he showed potential and the Twins knew he could become an elite hitter, injuries forced his release. Signing with the Boston Red Sox rejuvenated his career and sent him down the potential Hall of Fame path that he is currently on.

Ortiz broke out in his first year in Boston, hitting 31 home runs and driving in 101 runs as the Red Sox made it to just one game away from a World Series berth. The next year, Ortiz was a major part of the Red Sox team that broke the famed "Curse of the Bambino" and won the World Series for the first time since 1918. After a huge regular season, Ortiz hit a walk-off home run to win the Division Series and followed that up with another walk-off homer as the Sox held off elimination in Game 4 of the ALCS against the Yankees. He delivered another walk-off hit in the next game, giving the Sox all the momentum they needed to make their historic comeback from three games down.

He has continued to hit homers and drive in runs at a fearsome pace, showing no signs of slowing down. Though his 2012 season was cut short due to injury, Ortiz still bashed 23 home runs. He hit the 400-homer milestone this year and it will be no surprise if one of baseball's most popular players reaches 500 before his career is over.

The Detroit Tigers had swept their way through the ALCS, but timely hitting—and the arms of two Cy Young winners—from the San Francisco Giants led to a World Series sweep. After Pablo Sandoval hit home runs in his first three at-bats of the series, the rout was on.